Humpy the Moose

ISBN 10: 0-8280-0433-1
ISBN 13: 978-0-8280-0433-6

Printed in U.S.A.

Humpy the Moose

A Classic Story
Written and Illustrated
by Harry J. Baerg

REVIEW AND HERALD® PUBLISHING ASSOCIATION
HAGERSTOWN, MD 21741-1119

MOLLY, the cow moose, splashed through a swampy valley of northern British Columbia. She stared one way and then another, looking for something.

It was June in the mountains. Swamp buttercups and Indian paintbrush blossomed all around. The moose did not look at them or notice the sweet-smelling air. Thrushes, song sparrows, and redwings sang from the bushes, but she did not seem to hear them.

Sniffing the air, she raised her head and ran through the trees. There, at the opening of the woods, she saw it.

H. BAERG

SHE NOW STOOD at the edge of a lake. The water was still. Tall evergreen trees were reflected in it, and distant forest-covered hills and mountains showed through the misty air. Molly saw an island near the middle of the lake. It was covered with slender spruces. Water lilies grew near the shore.

The moose listened, and tested the air again with her nose. When everything looked safe, she stepped into the water and swam toward the island. There she shook the water out of her coat and disappeared into the brush.

NEXT DAY a little long-legged moose tried to stand up beside Molly. This was Humpy. He was getting his first look at the world about him. Ferns and bushes almost hid him in their leafy shade. Looking up, he saw the bright yellow-green tips of the hemlocks against the dark of the old needles and of the trunks of the trees.

A Canada jay, also called a moose-bird, peeked gently down from a branch and seemed to be surprised. Here was a baby moose not even a day old and yet it could stand up all by itself. The jay's young ones would have to be fed in the nest for weeks before they would be able to get about or fly.

BUT HUMPY was not yet able to take care of himself. He had to hide by the mossy log under the berry bushes while his mother was out feeding on the lilies. He saw many wonderful things as he lay there. Bees and butterflies flew from flower to flower and sometimes even lighted on him.

Once a rabbit hopped right beside him and ate without seeing him. Most animals see only things that move, and Humpy lay perfectly still. When he was still, no scent came from him, and the bunny's twitching nose could not smell him. Even a wolf or bear would have had a hard time finding him.

In a few days Humpy was scampering after his mother in the woods and tasting some of the plants she was eating.

HUMPY GREW FAST. In a little more than a month his mother decided that he could run and jump well enough to see more of the world with her. She had chosen the island as his first home because wolves or bears were less likely to be there to bother them. These were enemies they needed to watch for in the deep forest. Men also came there in the autumn to hunt.

Humpy and his mother had already eaten most of the fresh leaves and water lilies around the island, so now Molly led her son into the water, and they swam for the shore.

H. BAERG

ON THE MAINLAND the two moose found plenty of food. They liked leaves best of all. Their legs were so long that it was hard for them to reach the grass anyway. Where beavers had cut down poplar trees many young shoots grew around the stumps, and their juicy leaves were easy to reach. Later in summer, when the lower leaves had all been eaten, Humpy had to stand on his hind legs to reach the ones left. Sometimes Molly would walk over a small tree and bend it down to get at the leaves.

Humpy knew very little about the big world. As far as he knew, he and his mother were the only moose in it. But he was soon to find out otherwise.

ONE AUTUMN NIGHT while the two moose were peacefully chewing their cud, they heard a loud call. It came from across a stream near the lake. Humpy did not know what it was, but his mother did. She acted pleased, for it was a moose calling.

Autumn is the time of year when the father moose tries to find a mate, and sometimes there is a lot of fighting when two are after the same cow moose. Molly waited until the bull moose called again; then she answered and ran into the woods. Humpy followed, puzzled. If she answered, why did she run away?

FAR AWAY they heard a splash, then a crashing sound in the woods that sounded louder and nearer. Then a huge bull moose burst out of the bushes into an open space near them.

He stopped and stared around in the moonlight. Surely the call had come from somewhere near here. He raised his head and sniffed the air from side to side, then lifted his upper lip and snorted. Humpy saw moonlight shining on the sharp points of his large antlers, which looked like flattened tree branches fastened together.

HUMPY WAS AFRAID of the huge creature and stayed behind his mother, but his mother slowly slipped out of the dark woods. The bull saw her and snorted again. Then he trotted eagerly toward her. Now, shy again, Molly ran off into the woods. With many a snort and rumble the big moose followed her. After a while she allowed him to catch up, and the two became friends.

The bull followed Molly for several days. Humpy tried to be friends too, but the big moose hardly looked at him. He would have run over Humpy if the little fellow had not jumped out of the way.

ANOTHER DAY while the three were together they again heard a loud call. The bull's answer soon brought another bull moose. Molly's mate lunged at him. Soon the woods echocd with fierce clashes as their antlers crashed together. The two were evenly matched, but finally one of the bulls pierced the head of the other. When he tried to pull away he couldn't, for their antlers were locked together.

Humpy and his mother watched the hopeless struggle for a while. Then toward evening they heard a heavy animal moving in the brush. Molly sniffed, and then she and Humpy ran quietly out of the way.

H. BAERG

A GRIZZLY BEAR lumbering through the woods had heard the noise the bull moose had been making. When he found what had happened, he gave a low growl. The with a roar he rushed at the struggling moose. The live bull tried to face him, but he was helpless, and in the short struggle that followed he was the loser.

Humpy and his mother watched from a distance as the bear began a feast that was to fatten him for his sleep through the coming winter. There was plenty for not only him to eat, but also the wolves, foxes, crows, and jays for days to come.

THAT WINTER Humpy and his mother found much less food than they had in the summer, but they managed to stay alive on buds of aspen, alder, and willow trees. They also ate fir needles and stripped the bark from poplars with their lower front teeth. The long legs of the moose were now useful in walking through the deep snow.

One day two hungry timber wolves wallowed by through the soft snow near where the moose were feeding. Humpy crowded close to his mother, but he did not need to worry. The two wolves were having a hard time in the soft snow and were afraid to attack a grown moose alone. A better time for hunting would come later.

NEXT SPRING Humpy's mother chased him away. Though he was quite large he still wanted to follow her, but she struck at him with her front hoofs time after time. Once when he awoke from a nap he could not find her anywhere. He tried to follow her tracks and found that they ended at the shore of the lake. She was soon to have another calf and did not want him around. That was why she left him and hid again on the island where he had been born.

Humpy was quite unhappy about the way his mother had treated him, but he soon found that he could manage fairly well by himself.

THAT SUMMER Humpy grew soft little antlers that were all covered with velvet and had sharp points with which he could protect himself. The next summer he grew forked antlers.

By this time he was nearly full grown. He had become fat and sleek, and felt well able to look after himself. His ears and big rubber nose warned him of enemies, so he was able to keep away from them. He found, though, that some of his worst enemies were very small ones. From them he could not hide.

THESE WERE THE MOSQUITOES and no-see-ums. They could not kill Humpy, but they could make life miserable for him. Thousands of insects covered his coat, crawled into his ears and eyes, and made bumps on his tender nostrils where they bit him.

While eating lilies in the water Humpy would duck under and lose them for a short time, but he could not stay under water all the time. Later, on the bank, he felt like scratching his hide, so he rolled in the mud. This made him look very dirty, but the mud dried on like an armor and kept the insects off parts of him.

IN THE AUTUMN the young moose became restless again and wandered far from home. One moonlit night he heard a bugling call, as he had two years ago. He remembered and did not answer, but went closer. As he came to the shore of the river he heard the call again, and this time he heard an answer from a low hill nearby.

Humpy stood quietly and watched while the call came again. Something was wrong with the call from the river. He was not sure what it was. His eyes dimly saw an object on the water. It did not look like a moose, and seemed to be perfectly still. Maybe it was drifting slowly toward the shore.

THE BULL MOOSE did not answer anymore, and Humpy thought he had gone away, but suddenly Humpy saw him on the open beach. He pranced this way and that, looking for the cow moose he thought he had heard calling.

Humpy looked at the dark shape on the water and saw something move. Then a flash showed, and a loud, sharp noise like a breaking tree broke the stillness of the night. Looking again at the bull on the shore, Humpy saw him slowly sink to the ground, kick, and lie still. What had happened? There had been no fight, and yet the big moose was dead!

HUMPY WAS UNEASY though well hidden. Still, he was so curious about what had happened that he watched on. A shout came from the dark shape on the water. Then it came quickly to the shore. There part of the shape stayed at the water's edge and part moved toward the dead moose. After a while it moved back to the long object on the water with part of the moose, and went away.

This was Humpy's first meeting with man. Here was an enemy, though smaller than he was, that could kill at a distance with a stick that flashed and made noise. He backed into the forest and ran far away.

AS THE YEARS PASSED BY, Humpy grew larger and became wiser in many ways. He now stood seven feet tall at the shoulder and weighed as much as a horse. His shovel-like antlers spread to six feet between the outer points. Now as he stood in the pond his dark-brown coat shone in the sun. He heard the loons calling from the water and saw the ducks swimming nearby. Beavers worked hard at cutting down trees and building up their homes. Life was good to him, especially in the summer and fall.

WITH THE COMING of late fall and early winter Humpy found that he needed to be more careful again. In the summer there were few men in his part of the world, but in the autumn they came in to hunt, and he needed to keep out of reach of their guns. Because of what he had seen and heard that moonlit night on the riverbank, he was now very watchful.

Once day his sharp ears heard the faint sound of footsteps breaking the snow behind him. A hunter? He could not be sure until he had seen and smelled him. Walking fast around a small hill, he hid behind a bush where he could see his own tracks in the hollow below.

H. BAERG

FROM HIS HIDING PLACE Humpy saw and smelled a man with a gun. He was following the tracks, looking closely at them and then up to see where they were leading.

When the hunter was out of sight, humpy quietly rose and slipped away in the opposite direction. As soon as he was out of hearing he ran for the deeper woods.

The hunter following the tracks wondered why they would go in a circle. When he saw what the moose had done, he knew he was tracking a smart animal. He knew too that this moose was far away and that he had better start looking for another.

H. BAERG

AFTER THAT SCARE Humpy ran for a long time without stopping. Miles away in the deep forests of the endless hills he slowed down. Here he remained till the hunting season was over. By then it was midwinter, and the hunters were all gone.

With the hunters away, his main worry was the wolves. They had not been able to catch many deer or rabbits in the soft snow, but they had fed on the bodies of moose and deer left by hunters. Now the pair of timber wolves with their three grown cubs were hunting far and wide for food.

THAT WINTER the snow fell day after day and lay deep on the ground. Even Humpy with his long legs had trouble wading through. Then one day the sun shone warmly, melting the top of the snow until it was heavy with water. At night it grew cold again and froze hard, but not quite hard enough for Humpy. His sharp hoofs would break through, and then his knees would have to break the crust again coming up. In the woods where the sun had not melted the snow it was still soft, but in the open the crust was so hard that the moose often found it easier to jump than walk.

HUMPY was crossing the frozen lake through the crusted snow one day in search of food. He was having a hard time breaking through the snow and was getting tired. Halfway across he stopped to rest. Suddenly he thought he heard something behind him. While breaking the snow he had been making too much noise himself to hear it. But now, as he turned his large antlered head and trumpet ears in that direction, he clearly heard something that gave him quite a scare. Usually he would not have been so upset by it, but now that the snow was making it so hard for him to travel, he knew that he was in trouble, and was not sure what to do.

WOLVES WERE HOWLING on the hills above the lake. They were too far away from him to tell how many there were, but it was likely the family of five he had seen several times before. Maybe others had joined them and made the pack bigger. While the snow was soft they had been able to catch little other than a tired fox or coyote, so now they were very hungry. They ran lightly over the frozen snow of the open hillside while Humpy struggled heavily through the crust far from the shore. The wolves were large, and there were enough of them so that they were not afraid to attack. Humpy knew he would now have to fight for his life.

HUMPY HEADED for the shore in great leaps. It was hard work, and at times he had to slow down. On the shore of the lake he could see some large snow-covered rocks, and he plunged toward them. As soon as the wolves came out onto the open lake and saw the moose, their howling became quick and sharp. They dashed over the snow faster than ever. It looked hopeless for Humpy with the wolves rapidly closing in on him. Just as he reached the rocky shore, the leading wolf snapped at his heels. Humpy turned to face him and backed between the large mounds. The wolves snapped at him and tried to get at his hind legs, but he kept his head toward his enemies.

NOW THE REAL BATTLE began. The moose's head was down, and all his gleaming antler points were facing the wolves. They stopped and wondered how to attack. They tried scaring him out of his spot, but he would not leave. Some made believe they were attacking on one side while the rest tried to rush in on the other. Always the big head with antler points faced them. Humpy's hoofs could cut dangerously, and the wolves did not dare to come too close. They tried going away in the hope that he would leave his strong fort, but he knew better than to do so. The snow was becoming packed, and that was also in Humpy's favor. Finally the wolves became more hungry and bold.

AT LAST ONE OF THE WOLVES, bolder than the rest, came too close. Humpy caught him on his antlers and tossed him over his shoulder. Another came too near his hind legs and got a kick, which broke some bones. This made the wolves even more careful again.

Soon hunger made them rush in again. Humpy was ready for them. A sharp blow with his front foot put another wolf out of business, and a toss with his antlers reminded another to stay away. Now two wolves were dead, another soon would be, and a fourth was badly battered. Only the mother of the cubs was unhurt. She was about ready to leave, for this moose was more than they could handle.

JUST THEN HUMPY HELPED her to decide by boldly charging at the two wolves. With tails between their legs they raced across the lake. Surely there must be some food they could find that would be easier to catch than this moose!

Humpy, still very angry, stamped the other wolves into the snow and excitedly picked them up and tossed them with his antlers. He pranced back and forth over his battlefield till he was sure there was no more danger for him. Slowly his anger left him.

THEN THE VICTORIOUS HUMPY marched proudly, still trembling with excitement, into the woods where the snow was softer and not so deep. Here he stopped to rest. He calmed down slowly, and a feeling of peace came over him again. He had always lived at peace with the world about him, and it was not natural for him to fight as he had been doing. But when enemies threatened to take his life, he would and could fight. Now he looked out again over his hills and valleys, master of all he could see.